Journey 21

*21 Days, 10 Strategies
to a better Work Lfe*

Gail DePriest, MA

Affecting the quality of the day is the highest of the arts.
Thoreau

Contents

Introduction

At a recent gathering of human resource professionals from various corporations the issue of soft skills came up. Leaders spoke candidly about the importance of having employees who know how to manage themselves and their relationships with others. As organizations become leaner and employees are called upon to perform a variety of functions, it becomes more important for them to work well together and depend on one another for success. Developing soft skills allows for smoother interactions between employees and most likely will have a positive effect on the following:

Productivity: Softs skills contribute to productivity by helping individual stay in an emotional "toward" state – working proactively rather than reactively – and by building stronger relationships, enhancing collaboration and increasing accountability.

Psychological Well-being: Soft skills contribute to well-being by encouraging social support, reducing stress and helping employees align their actions with their values.

Retention and Employee Satisfaction: Employees who have sense of psychological well-being at work feel supported and safe and do not tend to leave this type of culture.

As organizations seek competitive advantage in the workplace, groups of fully engaged employees can spell the difference between success and failure. Because of this organizations are seeking new models and best practices so as to better support employees, gain their best contributions and retain them for the long haul.

You may have seen the recent Time Magazine cover entitled "The Mindfulness Revolution." Corporations such as Apple, Medtronic, Aetna, Google and Goldman Sachs are offering mindfulness classes to calm negative energies and help employees focus on creating innovative products. Some have set up dedicated meditation rooms within the workplace as a symbol of their company's commitment to mindfulness and creativity.

Aside from increasing innovative ideas, practicing mindfulness may also have a positive impact on their healthcare costs over time. When you consider that the use of practices like meditation, reflection and journaling are contributing to the success of many organizations, maybe we should all be taking a look.

What these organizations understand is the intense pressure their employees experience every day. They understand the need for employees to have more time to reflect so they can create ways to overcome difficult challenges. We are all challenged to find ways of sorting through our various daily demands and distractions so that we can achieve more clarity when making important decisions, more creativity in our work and more compassion for our colleagues and clients.

To address these issues, The Journey Project began as an effort to support MBA students and corporate employees with exercises in mindfulness, reflection and structured journaling as well as placing attention on strategic behaviors. This ten-step process challenges you to think about how you are managing yourself, how you are helping others to succeed and how you are adding value at work.

Management and leadership research in the past few decades has significantly enhanced our understanding of human workplace behavior and with the recent emergence of neuroscience, the benefits of soft skills are now supported by hard data. For the past two years we have empowered MBA students to use the latest brain science to prioritize their work more effectively with better allocation of brain resources. Our work has been informed by the new field of neuroleadership which allows for better decision making, facilitation of change and personal interactions.

As part of their educational experience, our MBA students were given a framework that directed their attention on three areas:

- Strategies for mindfulness, personal renewal and staying positive,

- Methods of supporting others through coaching, compassion and perspective-taking,

- And tools for contributing more effectively at work such as solutions-focus and creativity methodologies.

Students were asked to complete daily entries in a structured journal which provided them regular introspective practice so that they can move away from their routines and reflect on their work and life. Our hope was that students would cultivate daily practices that would allow our students to regularly renew themselves – taking skills with them to be more successful, happier and more fulfilled in the long run. What did MBA students say about the experience?

"I am nearly certain this leadership class might be the single most important course of my MBA journey. My perspective on how I can contribute to the workplace has taken on a whole new dimension, one that will be much more fulfilling,"

–BMW Engineer

"This program helped me to focus on what I needed to do and to keep a positive attitude throughout the day. I used the daily questions with my

employees at work: what went well today? What wish do you have for tomorrow? As a manager I was able to better understand what motivated them and what they enjoyed doing most."

–H. Worthington

"Adding one more thing to my to-do list seemed daunting at first, however, the insight and self discovery it provided proved invaluable. I have learned to use mindfulness to clear my head before a meeting and focus my thoughts has been extremely advantageous!"

–C. Moyer

With recent advances in brain science we know that neuroplasticity allows the brain to change according to where we place our attention. By keeping a log for at least 21 days you will begin to more readily sort for the positive each day allowing you to see greater possibilities and experience increased appreciation for the good things in your life and career. Research has shown that positive people are about 30% more productive at work.

Journey 21 is a culmination of our work in this field and we offer it to anyone who would like to journey with us. Take the *Journey 21* Challenge by committing 21 days to this project for your own personal growth at work.

You will find insights from cognitive neuroscience as well as positive psychology and appreciative inquiry (strengths and solutions) and also practical applications to use immediately at work – whatever kind of work you do.

How to Use This Book

The Daily Checklist

This is a structured journal that requires time in the morning and evening. Plan to give yourself approximately 10 minutes first thing in the AM and 10 minutes before bed to review and complete the daily checklist. Completing the checklist on a consistent basis allows you to form a positive habit by reinforcing the following things on a daily basis:

1. What went well allows you to relive something positive that happened during the day.

2. Acknowledging three things every day for which you are grateful brings you back to the positive.

3. Ten minutes of exercise is a reminder that your behavior matters and small changes can have big impact (at least 10 minutes of daily exercise).

4. The importance of daily meditation (or prayer) – insight arises when the brain is calm.

5. Positive affirmation of someone else by performing an act of kindness each day provides a boost in dopamine for yourself and someone else at work.

6. Engaging in visualization by posting a wish for tomorrow, which allows the brain to "see" a positive outcome and begin to use both conscious and unconscious resources to support that outcome.

Strategies for a Better Work Life

Strategies for a Better Work Life describes and gives examples of selected positive behaviors. You will choose a behavioral strategy to use each day and focus on that positive behavior all day. This is an experimental assignment that allows you to be in charge of how you use this strategic behavior. After twelve days you will have used all the strategies and can begin to incorporate multiple strategies into your day. Field assignments are provided along with supporting science.

Part 1
The Daily Checklist

The Daily Checklist

Complete this checklist every day for at least 21 days in a row.

Morning

Post three things you are grateful for today:

1

2

3

Select one behavioral strategy from Part 2 to use today and post here.

Get at least ten minutes of exercise today.

Take at least five minutes of quiet meditation and/or prayer today.

Perform a random act of kindness today and post here:

Evening

What one thing went well today?

What one wish do you have for tomorrow?

Part 2

Behavioral Strategies for a Better Work Life

Self, Beyond Self & Adding Value

Section 1: Self

The ability to manage self when working with others is critical. Having a sense of self-control is necessary in order to make good decisions, stay present in the moment and remain positive. But how is this possible when working in a chaotic environment? We introduce the following topics with supporting case studies and brain science.

Our wish for the reader is to honor instinct, practice self-control and use brain science for taking care of self and keeping a positive attitude. With technology streaming 24/7, the ability to hear one's instinct/inner voice can be difficult; yet according to brain science principles, insight comes from a calm brain.

Taking time to quiet the brain through meditation and centering is desirable and can be scheduled into the busiest of days. Mindfulness allows the brain to be present and more intentional about where to place attention. Self-control is necessary for creating rituals that allow time for reflection and introspection. With the ups and downs and daily stresses, staying positive can be challenging.

Topics included in this section are the following:

Mindfulness: Meditation for Centering

Renewal: Self-control is a Limited Resource

Positivity: Fostering a Sense of Optimism

Mindfulness: Being Present

What is it?

Mindfulness is being fully present in the moment with a non-judgmental acceptance of thoughts and feelings.

In Brief

With more and more information streaming at you 24/7, your ability to stay in the moment is challenged and you are probably just trying to manage the constant flow. You may also find that it is hard to stay focused on the project or the meeting you are in. Taking some time to follow your breathing will allow you to relax and tap into your most creative self. In a state of distraction, too many things are going on and your attention to any of them is fragmented. It is important that you have a tool for clearing your mind and it can make all the difference for you as you try to manage the many tasks of your day.

Case Study

Maria is an Ob-gyn practicing in a metropolitan city. She and her two colleagues are wonderful caregivers to women from the moment they share the good news about their pregnancy all the way through to the birth of their child. Maria was tireless in her role as a compassionate caregiver but she was also very energized by the all the positive feedback and appreciation from her patients. After ten years of practice she was offered the position of Chief Medical Officer at her hospital.

This new role was exciting and offered her a chance to learn so much more, however, the new role required the use of new competencies – reviewing financials, improving the quality numbers and being part of an executive team. She found herself getting emotional, feeling frustrated and even defensive. She had never felt so much pressure in her career – not even in the delivery room! Maria was given an executive coach and began to work on some new outcomes that she desired for herself. She implemented a plan that required her to connect with herself throughout the day. She made time to stop and follow her breath between meetings. She made time to do some mindful walking. She felt a reduction in her stress whenever she remembered to breath. She visualized outcomes she wanted to see for the day and carefully prioritized her schedule. Now she speaks to other health care practitioners about the importance of practicing mindfulness.

Reflection

Have you experienced a time when you were feeling overwhelmed and frustrated at work? How were you able to reach a state of calm?

Related Research

The practice of mindfulness is increasingly being linked to a wide variety of positive outcomes, including emotion regulation, reduced stress and improved psychological well-being. A practice of mindfulness can also help avoid conflict by early detection of problems as well as identify opportunities that might have otherwise been missed.

Behavioral Strategies

Field Assignment

Find a place in nature or somewhere quiet to practice deep breathing. Follow your breath…letting go of thoughts of judgment. If you would like, close your eyes and visualize a place you enjoy: the beach, the mountains, the park near your home...

Keep your eyes closed as you continue to follow your breath. Experience all the sensory aspects of this location: the smells, the sounds, the breeze on your face, the relaxation you feel in your body...

Imagine letting go of all fears and anxieties as you sit very still, watching them float into space and dissipate in the clouds. Feel sunshine streaming into your body from your head to your toes.

Breathe in, holding your breath for a moment and slowly releasing.

If you like, repeat a word or phrase over and over with your breathing or alternately you may want to use a favorite prayer.

Set your cell timer so that you may relax without checking time.

Debrief
Did this exercise help you to get calm and centered? What might have worked better?

What are some specific situations where you might use this technique?

Interview an Inspiring Individual
Develop other strategies for handling stress and frustration by interviewing someone who has mastered the ability to stay calm at work.

Further Reading
Farb, N., et al. (2007). Attending to the present: mindfulness meditation reveals distinct neural modes of self-reference. Social, Cognitive and Affective Neuroscience, 2, 313-322.

Tang, Y.Y., et al. (2007). Short-term meditation training improves attention and self-regulation. Proc. Natl. Acad. Sci. U. S. A.

Renewal: Self-Control Is a Limited Resource

What is it?

Renewal is the deliberate act of building up inner resources to support acts of both physical and emotional self-control.

In Brief

Self-control for renewal or nurturing self is increasingly important in today's work environment. Have you ever had time at work when you became so caught up in your work that you did not take care of yourself? Perhaps you were working towards a deadline or working many hours to complete a project. You were probably mentally and physically exhausted and in need of renewal. Renewal or nurturing self requires self-control and planning. Exercising self-control in this way will be beneficial to you and those around you. Making the time to step away from the work, go for a short walk, do something nice for yourself or someone else will renew you and refresh you for returning to your work.

Case Study

Amy worked for a global consulting firm, having responsibility for the business operations in her region. She was a very bright, successful woman, building a reputation for herself as very innovative and resourceful. After several years in her role, Amy was promoted to a corporate director position in which she was to launch a new business line for the organization.

She was delighted to be recognized for her innovative work with clients and very pleased that she would be reporting into the executive team at the corporate office. Since she would be responsible for the entire U.S., Amy's new job put her on planes, flying day in and day out to almost every meeting. She quickly found that she was overbooking her schedule and became increasingly exhausted. Her new schedule required a different kind of self nurturing and she knew that she needed to make adjustments. Amy knew that taking care of herself on the road should include a reduction in meetings as well as scheduling time for rest and exercise. After making this change, she became much more effective at her meetings and closing deals because her energy was better and she was able to prepare more effectively.

Reflection

Have you experienced a time when you were not taking care of yourself at work – not getting the renewal you need to be at your best?

Related Research

For more than a decade researchers have been studying self-control or willpower as a limited resource that can be depleted through use. That is, performing an act of self-control reduces existing resources and impairs future acts of self-control unless the resource is replenished. Studies have found effective means of replenishment include consuming glucose, acts that induce positive mood, practicing self affirmation exercises and resting.

Behavioral Strategies

Field Assignment

Rituals for renewal are events that we put in place on a regular basis – those things that we do for and with ourselves to honor what is important and help replenish resources.

Which of the following rituals might help you move forward and reach your goals – specifically ones that you will enjoy and want to keep and honor?

Getting up at an earlier hour?

Setting aside time for planning?

Setting time for reflection and writing?

Walking to clear your head ?

Meeting with an accountability partner?

Establishing a discovery date with yourself to explore something new?

Scheduling an hour each week to revisit your vision and tweak the details?

Apply this strategy by selecting at least one of the above and practicing it on a regular basis.

Debrief

How well did it work for you? What could have been better?

What are some specific situations where you might apply this information?

Interview an Inspiring Individual

Develop other strategies by interviewing someone who has mastered the ability to stay renewed.

Suggested Reading

Ackerman, J.M., et al. (2009). You wear me out: The vicarious depletion of self-control. Psychological Science, 20(3), 326-332.

Egan, P., et al. (2012). Taking a fresh perspective: Vicarious restoration as a means of recovering self-control. Journal of Experimental Social Psychology,48, 457-465.

Positivity: Fostering a Sense of Optimism

What is it?

Positivity is an attitude that focuses attention on the pathways to success instead of dwelling on negativity that can cause stress, fear and blame.

In Brief

Many workers feel isolated and even left out at work. The very nature of some office workflow and leadership styles can lead to this. Take the time to make connections with co-workers – for yourself and for them. What are the benefits of focusing on positivity? Staying focused on the positive increases your sense of gratitude for all that is good. An increased sense of gratitude allows you to bring about more of what you are seeking. Ever heard the expression, "what you think about is what you bring about?" We often tend to focus on what is not going well and we lose sight of what is working, what is successful.

Case Study

Jim had a new boss and was looking forward to working with him. He had heard good things and was expecting to build a great relationship. Jim met with the new boss and began the process of managing up. What Jim was to find out over the next several weeks is that his new boss had a leadership style in which he communicated to team members mostly on a one-to-one basis assuring that the team as a whole usually did not know what was happening.

Most of them felt they weren't important enough to be included in the inner circle and yet there wasn't an inner circle - just poor or spotty communication. Jim realized that he had to take responsibility for creating positivity for himself and potentially others, too. He thought about the expression "what you think about you bring about," and he started to focus on the things that were going well on this team. The boss wasn't a strong communicator and morale was low but Jim decided he would keep himself positive and intentionally encouraged others as he could. In time he found that it made him more able to cope with the uncertainty that comes in an environment where one can feel left out and uninformed.

Reflection

When was a time you had to remain positive in a difficult situation?

Related Research

Fostering a sense of optimism usually involves priming the brain to look for the positive. What about the days that are just plain horrible? The revolutionary news is that positive thinking changes the brain in a real physical way – neuroplasticity. Our thoughts can change the structure and function of the brain. Williams James suggested this in 1890 but he was soundly dismissed by scientists who believed the brain is rigidly mapped out. Turns out they were wrong. Neuroplasticity enjoys wide acceptance as scientists are now saying the brain is adaptable and dynamic. It has the power to change structure – even for people who have had a stroke or mental illness.

Behavioral Strategies

Field Assignment

Gratitude has been linked to improved psychological well-being, supportive social behavior such as sharing and cooperating, and positive relationships. This activity helps to develop gratitude by turning attention to aspects of life you are grateful for, as well as reframing negative situations into positive and meaningful opportunities.

1. Identify a time and location that will allow you to have a few moments of uninterrupted focus on the task at hand.

2. Set a timer for sixty seconds and make a list of anything you are grateful for in your life. Write the ideas as they flow into your mind. Write the ideas without judging or thinking about them.

3. When the time is up, reflect on your list. What could you be doing to enhance or acknowledge the things you are grateful for in your life? For example, if you are grateful for a person, how might you enhance this relationship?

4. Consider one situation or event that you currently view in a negative manner and attempt to positively reframe it so that it becomes meaningful and valuable. For example, you may choose to view a seemingly negative situation as a chance to learn, begin a new career path, develop self awareness or enrich a relationship.

5. What actions might you take to make this reframed perspective a reality for you?

Debrief

How was the experience helpful? When might your use this technique?

When you practice positivity, you model the way for others around you. Make a habit of noticing the reactions of others when you purposely make an effort to stay positive in a difficult situation and use this feedback to guide future efforts.

Suggested Reading

Lambert, N. M., et al. (2009). A changed perspective: How gratitude can affect sense of coherence through positive reframing. Journal of Positive Psychology, 4, 461-470.

Section 2: Beyond Self

Corporations and other organizations have said that technical skills only take an employee so far. Leadership is more than getting ahead; it also consists of helping others to find opportunities and success.

It is our hope that the reader will become more aware of the needs of others and their desire for support, appreciation, and acknowledgement. You can support others by showing compassion and empowering them through planned, specific praise.

These are desirable tools for a leader, but sometimes the last thing on the mind of an individual who wants to make their mark in the corporate world.

Topics include in this section include:

Appreciation: Empowering Others Through Praise

Coaching: Supporting Others in Achieving Goals

Compassion: Showing that you Care

Perspective Taking: Walking in their Shoes

Appreciation: Empowering Others Through Praise

What is it?

Showing appreciation is a tangible signal that someone else's contributions are valued.

In Brief

The ability to offer genuine and specific acts of appreciation is a powerful tool in the development of strong relationships and productive collaboration with others. Feeling appreciated affirms a sense of belonging, and can nurture a positive mental state supporting higher productivity and creativity. Use appreciation when you want to affirm someone at work. Most people agree it is a good thing to do but many of us are awkward at doing it. Becoming better at the art of showing appreciation will bring appreciation and gratification back to you and empower your colleague or employee.

Case Study

Sarah was a young graphic designer just getting started in her first professional job. She had held a number of internships throughout the years but now she was named Manager of Graphic Communication for her organization. She was eager to get started, work with her team and make a contribution. Her new organization was a highly visible entity having interaction with many businesses throughout the region. After several weeks in her new role, she shared with her mother that her most proud moment was when her boss noticed her work and thanked her for the great job she was doing

She immediately began taking more pride in the overall production. She thought she was doing nice work but to have her boss specifically offer comments about some of her designs and to thank her for the special efforts she had made was very empowering to her. Soon after this she enrolled in another design class and began to hone her skill to a new level. She also made a point to show her appreciation to her co-workers knowing how good it had made her feel to be noticed and appreciated.

Reflection

When was a time that someone showed you appreciation for your work? How did it make you feel?

Related Research

Appreciation goes beyond recognition and is a powerful tool in the development of strong relationships and the productive collaboration with others. Feeling appreciated affirms the sense of belonging and can nurture a positive mental state supporting higher productivity and creativity.

Behavioral Strategies
Field Assignments

Awareness: Start by making a deliberate effort to notice small acts that you genuinely appreciate. It might be as specific as a person you want to improve a relationship with, or it might be general interactions with anyone you meet during the day.

Take Notes: Don't rely on your memory, because part of the strategy is to wait a few days before showing your appreciation. Approximately 3-5 days after you noticed the act you want to acknowledge, find a way to convey your appreciation statement to the recipient. If you are delivering the message in person, make eye contact and notice the reaction. If you convey the message electronically or by phone, consider adding more narrative to set up the appreciation statement and invite a response.

The more specific you can make your appreciation, the greater the impact.

Appreciation Statement: Using your notes, craft a statement of appreciation along the following structure: "I appreciate _____ because _____."

Example: I appreciate your patience with customers as you showed working with Mr. Jones last

Tuesday, because it makes them feel valued and boosts customer loyalty.

Debrief

What happened? What could be improved?

Identify at least one situation where you may use this strategy in the future.

Interview an Expert/Acquaintance

Identify someone who has mastered the art of showing appreciation.

Suggested Reading

Lieberman, M. D. and Eisenberger, N. I. (2009). The pains and pleasures of social life. Science, Vol. 323(5916), pp. 890-891.

Coaching: Supporting Others in Achieving Goals

What is it?

Coaching is fast becoming a core leadership competency – a highly desired ability to support individuals to achieve goals, produce results, enhance performance and increase accountability.

In Brief

Have you ever had a great manager who would carefully listen to you, ask questions and make an effort to understand the problem you were facing, then offer thoughts and encouragement? You may have been coached. The best managers help you find your way so that you can grow your own skills in problem solving. A great coach will guide you but also wait and allow you to reach that "ah ha!" moment on your own by talking it through.

Business Case

Sam and Mike worked for a large university IT department and had known each other for some time. They occasionally ran into each other and talked about the issues they had in their particular areas of the school IT network. One spring they were asked to attend a leadership program for leaders in their department and came together for their first session. One of the exercises was for mock coaching, using a list of coaching questions.

Given the assignment to work together, they actually solved a problem they had discussed several times before. They came up with solutions that had not yet surfaced. Sam commented that he had been asking the wrong questions previously and was really just too busy telling Mike what to do rather than listening. It wasn't until he held back and let Mike process the problem out loud that Mike was able to solve it. A few question to help you start the coaching conversation:

- What do you hope to achieve and what will achieving this do for you?
- How will you know when you gotten there?
- How will others know when you have achieved this?
- How will this outcome affect other areas of your life?
- What stops you from doing this?
- What actions will you be taking between now and the next time we talk?
- When will you start?

Reflection

Was there a time that you would have benefited from coaching?

Research

Coaching allows space for listening and encouraging, while allowing the recipient to talk through an issue and get in a "toward" state of openness and curiosity.

A difficult challenge for a new coach is to avoid giving advice to the recipient or promote a solution they believe to be best. Brain science and common experience suggest that allowing someone to reach their own "aha!" moment of insight is more likely to create a "buy in" to the process of implementing a solution.

Behavioral Strategies

Field Assignment

Find a trusted partner who is willing to participate in a coaching practice session. Ask them to identify a challenge they would like to explore, and ask the basic coaching questions deliberately as they appear in the list without variation. While it may seem mechanical at first, this helps new coaches develop a foundation for future coaching sessions.

Have a coaching conversation with a direct report or colleague around a challenge they are currently facing. Once they identify the challenge, begin guiding them through the basic coaching questions and use the extended questions as appropriate.

After the session, reflect on your effectiveness by considering these questions:

- Did you adequately gather information to understand issue? (clarify)

- Did you express empathy in order to connect? (empathize)

- Did you guide the conversation toward problem solving? (question)

- Did you share in the strategy of problem solving - offering ideas or suggestion? (strategize)

- Did you help the recipient focus in on action items? (focus)

- Did you talk about a time frame for getting this done? (assess)

Debrief

Identify at least one situation where you may use this strategy.

Interview an Expert/Acquaintance

Identify someone who is an effective coach and interview them.

Suggested Reading

Ely, K. et al. (2010). Evaluating leadership coaching: A review and integrated framework. The Leadership Quarterly, 21, 585-599.

Rock, D. & Page, L. (2008). Coaching with the Brain in Mind: Foundations for Practice.

Compassion:
Showing That You Care

What is it?

Compassion is the ability to recognize someone else's suffering accompanied by the strong desire to alleviate the suffering.

In Brief

If you have ever experienced a moment when someone reached out to you to show compassion for your situation, you know how important compassion can be. Having a colleague or manager ask about your work load or a personal issue you are struggling with can make you feel incredibly supported - even make your problem seem more tolerable.

Case Study

In the midst of a large organizational restructuring, plant workers were feeling frustrated and even angry. Reductions in force had been made and one shift was actually shut down temporarily; most workers just didn't know what to expect from day to day. A woman named Ellen was the manager of almost 60 employees. Every day she was asked many questions for which she did not have answers. She had never expected anything like this when she accepted the role of manager. There was one thing she had plenty of and that was compassion. She knew it was hard for employees to be in the dark. She took the time to hear from each person who wanted to talk with her.

Reflection

When is a time that someone showed you compassion at work? How did it make you feel?

Related Research

Acting compassionately toward others paradoxically also increases self-compassion, which can provide surprising benefits. Although somewhat counter-intuitive, studies link self-compassion with an increased willingness to learn from and improve on self-perceived mistakes, failures or weaknesses. Whereas being strongly self-critical can over-activate the feeling brain and disrupt the productivity of the thinking brain, treating yourself with the same kindness you would treat a friend or child can actually boost motivation to achieve goals. Being self-compassionate does not lower standards as some might think; instead, it seems to provide much-needed support from within to help make it through the ups and downs of striving for a meaningful goal.

Self-compassion has yet another surprising benefit: it has been linked with increased creative originality, especially for people who tend to be overly critical of themselves. Since creativity demands a non-judgmental climate to flourish, it may be that self-critical individuals squash their new ideas before they have a chance to grow. Self-compassion, which includes a more accepting mind-set, may facilitate originality by providing a more nurturing environment for new ideas to develop before being rejected.

Behavioral Strategies
Field Assignment

Review each of the questions below and give yourself a point for each affirmative answer.

In the past week, have you:

Showed appreciation or encouragement to someone?

Asked someone how they were doing and actually listened with intent for understanding?

Noticed someone who could use a hand and made an effort to help out?

Made an effort to enrich a relationship?

Made an effort to visit and get to know someone outside your usual circle of acquaintances?

Made a deliberate attempt to show compassion to your own self?

___ Total Score

For each of the affirmative answers, what ripple effects might result?

What are three specific ways you could boost your score next week?

Debrief

Identify at least one situation where you may use this strategy.

Interview an Expert/Acquaintance

Identify someone who exhibits compassion and interview them.

Suggested Readings

Brienes, J. & Chen, S. (2012). Self-compassion increases self-improvement motivation. Personality and Social Psychology Bulletin, TBD.

Neff, K. D. (2009). Self-compassion. In M. R. Leary & R. H. Hoyle (Eds.), Handbook of individual differences in social behavior (pp. 561–573). New York, NY: Guilford Press.

Zabelina, D. & Robinson, M. (2010). Don't be so hard on yourself: Self-compassion facilitates creative originality among self-judgmental individuals. Creativity Research Journal, 22(3), 288 - 293.

Perspective Taking:
Walking in Their Shoes

What is it?

Perspective taking forms the basis for understanding the intentions of others by mentally putting yourself in someone else's shoes.

In Brief

If you are able to take others' perspectives into consideration you are much more likely to avoid conflict and find common ground for team solutions. Whatever your occupation, the skill of perspective taking will serve you well and improve your ability to do the following:

- Enable your direct reports to share with you.

- Be open to the input of others and collaborate more successfully.

- Deal with feelings and needs of others - both employees and customers.

- Put yourself in someone else's shoes, imagining their point of view.

- Use feedback to make necessary/recommended changes.

- Understand what others think before judging.

Case Study

Tom was the Vice President of Sales for his organization. He was constantly being harassed by the Sam the Chief Financial officer asking for tiny details and various types of reports and projections. It made his job much more complex because Sam created extra work for him and his team and at times when he least expected it! He began to feel that Sam was picking on him and the tension between them was growing. Tom began to work with an executive coach who encouraged him to work on key relationships within the executive team. This mean he would be spending some time with Sam to learn more about Sam's role and responsibilities. Tom found Sam to be reception to the idea and Sam began to share with Tom the type questions and demands that he received from the President and others on the board. Tom was surprised to know that Sam was really under the gun for so much information on a regular basis. He realized that Sam had been producing financial reports and forecasts for the board of directors sometimes at a moment's notice. Tom knew this on some level but had not realized the pressure Sam was under. Gaining this perspective allowed him to have a greater appreciation for the work Sam was doing and Tom began to work more collaboratively with him. It took walking in Sam's shoes for several hours and a few meetings to gain this perspective.

Reflection

When was a time you stepped back to consider another person's perspective? How did it help?

Related Research

Perspective taking calls on many of the executive functions of the brain. It requires inhibiting our own thoughts and feelings in order to consider the perspective of others. It requires cognitive flexibility to see a situation in different ways and the ability to consider someone else's thinking alongside your own.

Behavioral Strategies
Field Assignment

Think about a conflict you have experienced recently - whether it is with someone in your family or someone at work. Chances are that the inability to see things as others see them is at the heart of these problems. Make two separate lists showing how you and the other person may be viewing the same situation. Refrain from judgment as you are making both lists.

By accepting differences and seeking to value the uniqueness of the other person, we open up channels for collaboration. We focus a lot of time on sorting out our own feelings; equally important is appreciating diversity of thought. Ask yourself, did you make sure the other person felt heard, understood, and appreciated? Did you acknowledge what he/she was asking? Did you verify that you are clear on his/her request? This helps others know that their opinion is important and heard even if not acted upon.

How would you handle the same situation in the future? Could you use cognitive perspective taking to more fully understand the position of your colleague? What questions could you ask to gain more information and make sure you are actively listening?

Debrief

What went well? What could have been better?

Identify at least one situation where you can use this strategy.

Interview an Expert/Acquaintance

Identify someone who has mastered this principle and interview.

Suggested Readings

Bruneau, E. & Saxe, R. (2012) The power of being heard: The benefits of 'perspective giving' in intergroup conflict. Journal of Experimental Social Psychology, dpi:10.1016/j.jesp.2012.02.017.

Pillay, S.S. (2011). Your Brain and Business: The Neuroscience of Great Leaders. Pearson Education Inc.

Section 3: Adding Value

Corporations are hiring and promoting individuals who bring ideas and solutions to their workplace. Individuals who are able to effectively collaborate with others, in a positive spirit, while staying resilient during difficult times will be very valuable in the work force.

Accordingly, our wish for the reader is to approach work with a desire to stay aligned with the overall goals of his or her organization, to contribute and stay focused on best solutions, to be creative and innovative when appropriate, to remain resilient even during times of high stress, secure in the knowledge that the brain functions more effectively when able to prioritize.

Topics include:

>   Innovation: Creativity at Work
>
>   Resiliency: Bouncing Back
>
>   Solutions Focus: Looking Forward

Innovation: Creativity at Work

What is it?

Creative thinking is the process of generating new ideas, and innovation results from the practical application of a creative idea to add value in some way.

Business Case

In a 2010 IBM study with over 1500 executives worldwide, creativity was named the number one leadership attribute these CEOs most wanted in their employees. When creativity is applied at work we then call it innovation. It's a new day – we all need to be more innovative at work as we live in times that are much more competitive.

Case Study

Jim works for a large global manufacturing company. He had been thinking for some time that the boxes in his plant might be more valuable if they were repurposed in some way. Once they came into the plant and the contents were removed, they were recycled. He had an assignment in his MBA program to create an innovation project at work. He was challenged to do something that might increase revenue, decrease cost or improve morale. His mind went back to the boxes. What if...? He talked with boss the next morning and they had both been wondering the same thing. They decided to take some time and flip a few boxes. Once the boxes were flipped, they could be barcoded once again and sent out the door. They soon tallied up the savings of new boxes and everyone loved the "green" aspect of the project. Jim did not consider himself to be highly creative but his project was selected as one of the top three innovation at work contenders in his MBA program. His company projected they would save hundreds of thousands of dollars with this change in not one but two plants. Jim was pretty sure he would innovate again at work!

Reflection

Is there some value you could add at work by being more innovative?

How could you use your creativity to make a positive change?

Related Research

Creative thinking is the process of generating new ideas and innovation results from the practical application of a creative idea to add value in some way. There are several degrees of innovation: it may be small-scale such as showing appreciation to co-workers in a new way or incremental development of an existing produce to service or as large as a new product that disrupts existing business models. The pathway from creative idea to major innovative solution is typically chaotic and ill-defined.

Behavioral Strategies

Field Assignment

1. Brainstorm to generate at least ten creative ideas about ways to solve a challenge you are currently facing that is meaningful to you.

2. For this practice activity, choose the one that you believe is most original and surprising. Visualize with all senses engaged the impact your innovation solution might have.

3. Evaluate your idea including the following questions:
   How would it impact people, both directly and indirectly?
   What are the known facts related to the idea?
   What facts need to be discovered?
   What are the steps you might follow to implement the idea?

What can you learn from others (or other industries) who
have a similar challenge?

What might be a surprising or unintended consequence if
you implement this idea?

What negatives are associated with the idea and how
might you fix them?

4. Identify at least three experiments you could conduct to
    test out your idea in a low risk environment to learn more
    about the path to success.

5. Make a decision. Should it be implemented right away or
    put on the shelf for future consideration or discarded as
    a bad idea?

Debrief

Interview an Expert/Acquaintance

Identify someone who you consider to be innovative and
interview him or her.

Suggested Readings

Michalko, Michael, (2006) Thinkertoys: Handbook of Creative
Thinking Techniques, Ten Speed Press.

Michalko,Michael, (2001) Craccking Creativity: The Secrets of
Creative Genius, Ten Speed Press.

Resiliency: Bouncing Back

What is it?

Resiliency is the ability to bounce back from failures and setbacks.

In Brief

Most of us have had a job or project that took a great deal of
energy, keeping us up late and out early in the morning in pursuit
of our mission. Sometimes we are successful in our endeavors
and other times we have to endure failure. More often than
not, the biggest challenges come with difficulties, obstacles,
and frustrations! Sometimes situations are even painful and
disappointing after all our hard work. How do you keep your
resiliency?

Case Study

Ben and his brother Brandon wanted to start a small business.
They were both athletic coaches with day jobs so they worked
feverishly at night on their business plan and their preparations
to launch a small company manufacturing sportswear. They did
their research, they met with lenders and they found a potential
customer for their product! Finally they started producing
sportswear just like they had planned. They loved sports!

This was what they had always hoped for. After that first order,
however, they found that the market was somewhat saturated
for this type of product. They found themselves back at square
one. They had to regroup and determine their path forward.
They continued to work on the idea, to do their research, to
talk to many people until, one day a few years after their initial
start-up, they connected with a corporation that needed basic
uniforms. While they were not sure how they were going to do
it, they proposed and won that first order! They were determined
to make it happen no matter what they had to do and they were

successful. They maintained resiliency until they could uncover a market niche that they could fill.

Reflection

When was a time that you were able to bounce back – to stay resilient at a difficult time?

Related Research

In research about resilience, it was found that those individuals who are resilient consistently do three things: they accept the difficulty of the matter, they find meaning in what they are experiencing and they get creative about finding solutions.

Behavioral Strategies

Field Assignment

Describe a situation where you needed resiliency.

Were you able to:

- Accept the difficulty in the situation?

- Stare down the reality of the situation?

- Find some meaning in the situation?

- Discover a positive aspect to the situation?

- Be creative in the situation?

- Improvise a solution using your resources inventively?

- Find social support to reduce stress and increase resilience?

Debrief

What went well? What could have been better?

Identify at least one situation where you may use this strategy:

Interview an Expert/Acquaintance

Identify someone who is highly resilient and interview them.

Suggested Reading

Coutu, D. (2002). How resilience works. Harvard Business Review. May, 46-55.

Seligman, M. (2011). Building resilience: Failure. Recover from it. Harvard Business Review, April, 100-106.

Solutions Focus: Looking Forward

What is it?

Solutions focus means avoiding the pointless search for what causes problems and focusing instead on the path that leads to a solution.

In Brief

Keeping a solutions focus can be a tremendous challenge when there are many variables that exist beyond your control. It can be very easy to focus on what is not going well and lose sight of that which IS going well. Appreciative inquiry is a methodology that allows taking stock of the positive aspects of a situation so as to bring about more of what is working.

Case Study

Kirby knew he had a great deal of work ahead. Fortunately one thing he did exceptionally well was keeping a solutions focus. No matter what problem came up, he would ask himself and his staff, "how do we make this better going forward?" "What might we do differently for better results?" He remained positive and was consistently seeking solutions and getting his team in a "toward state." This is a state in which the brain starts seeking and providing options. At first the staff was quiet and hesitant to offer up ideas, however, under his calm demeanor the staff soon joined him in offering ideas and suggestions. He was beginning to create a safe space for them to do the discovery work often involved in exploring possible solutions. In no time he had everyone thinking about and implementing positive solutions on a regular basis. Needless to say the division has been very successful under his leadership.

Reflection

When is a time that you have been challenged to find solutions and new ways of doing things?

Were you able to ask the right questions to get others to join you in your search for answers?

Related Research

Having a solutions focus is a different way to approach problems and puts the focus on creativity and construction rather than laying blame. In other words, the focus is on the solution rather than the problems, the future rather than the past and what is going well, rather than what is going wrong.

Behavioral Strategies
Field Assignment

This approach primarily means finding out what works and doing more of it. As you think about issues you want to address, make sure you are focused on the following in your discussions:

- Solutions not problems.

- What do we want to achieve and what will it look like?

- How can you word your questions and conversation to get colleagues to open up about their vision for the situation, the best of what can be?

- Interaction and positive discussions are critical to the process.

- People want to be heard whether their idea is adopted or not.

- Be sure to honor the wisdom in the room.

When you are looking at a specific challenge, consider the following questions:

- What is good that should be kept?

- What can be salvaged?

- What possibilities exist – now and in the future?

- After exploring the core of what is already in place:

- What simply must go?

Identify at least one situation where you may use this strategy.

Debrief
Interview an Expert/Acquaintance

Identify someone who is highly competent in this principle and interview.

Suggested Readings.

Cooperrider, D. L. et al. (2008). Appreciative Inquiry Handbook: For Leaders of Change. Berrett-Koehler Publishers.

Cooperrider, D. L., & Whitney, D. (2008). A positive revolution in change: Appreciative inquiry. Berrett-Koehler Publishers.

The Daily Checklist Journal

The Daily Checklist

Complete this checklist every day for at least 21 days in a row.

Morning

Post three things you are grateful for today:

1

2

3

Select one behavioral strategy from Part 2 to use today and post here.

Get at least ten minutes of exercise today.

Take at least five minutes of quiet meditation and/or prayer today.

Perform a random act of kindness today and post here:

Evening

What one thing went well today?

What one wish do you have for tomorrow?

The Daily Checklist

Complete this checklist every day for at least 21 days in a row.

Morning

Post three things you are grateful for today:

1

2

3

Select one behavioral strategy from Part 2 to use today and post here.

Get at least ten minutes of exercise today.

Take at least five minutes of quiet meditation and/or prayer today.

Perform a random act of kindness today and post here:

Evening

What one thing went well today?

What one wish do you have for tomorrow?

The Daily Checklist

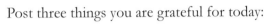

Complete this checklist every day for at least 21 days in a row.

Morning

Post three things you are grateful for today:

1

2

3

Select one behavioral strategy from Part 2 to use today and post here.

Get at least ten minutes of exercise today.

Take at least five minutes of quiet meditation and/or prayer today.

Perform a random act of kindness today and post here:

Evening

What one thing went well today?

What one wish do you have for tomorrow?

The Daily Checklist

Complete this checklist every day for at least 21 days in a row.

Morning

Post three things you are grateful for today:

    1

    2

    3

Select one behavioral strategy from Part 2 to use today and post here.

Get at least ten minutes of exercise today.

Take at least five minutes of quiet meditation and/or prayer today.

Perform a random act of kindness today and post here:

Evening

What one thing went well today?

What one wish do you have for tomorrow?

The Daily Checklist

Complete this checklist every day for at least 21 days in a row.

Morning

Post three things you are grateful for today:

1

2

3

Select one behavioral strategy from Part 2 to use today and post here.

Get at least ten minutes of exercise today.

Take at least five minutes of quiet meditation and/or prayer today.

Perform a random act of kindness today and post here:

Evening

What one thing went well today?

What one wish do you have for tomorrow?

The Daily Checklist

Complete this checklist every day for at least 21 days in a row.

Morning

Post three things you are grateful for today:

1

2

3

Select one behavioral strategy from Part 2 to use today and post here.

Get at least ten minutes of exercise today.

Take at least five minutes of quiet meditation and/or prayer today.

Perform a random act of kindness today and post here:

Evening

What one thing went well today?

What one wish do you have for tomorrow?

The Daily Checklist

Complete this checklist every day for at least 21 days in a row.

Morning

Post three things you are grateful for today:

    1

    2

    3

Select one behavioral strategy from Part 2 to use today and post here.

Get at least ten minutes of exercise today.

Take at least five minutes of quiet meditation and/or prayer today.

Perform a random act of kindness today and post here:

Evening

What one thing went well today?

What one wish do you have for tomorrow?

The Daily Checklist

Complete this checklist every day for at least 21 days in a row.

Morning

Post three things you are grateful for today:

1

2

3

Select one behavioral strategy from Part 2 to use today and post here.

Get at least ten minutes of exercise today.

Take at least five minutes of quiet meditation and/or prayer today.

Perform a random act of kindness today and post here:

Evening

What one thing went well today?

What one wish do you have for tomorrow?

The Daily Checklist

Complete this checklist every day for at least 21 days in a row.

Morning

Post three things you are grateful for today:

1

2

3

Select one behavioral strategy from Part 2 to use today and post here.

Get at least ten minutes of exercise today.

Take at least five minutes of quiet meditation and/or prayer today.

Perform a random act of kindness today and post here:

Evening

What one thing went well today?

What one wish do you have for tomorrow?

The Daily Checklist

Complete this checklist every day for at least 21 days in a row.

Morning

Post three things you are grateful for today:

    1

    2

    3

Select one behavioral strategy from Part 2 to use today and post here.

Get at least ten minutes of exercise today.

Take at least five minutes of quiet meditation and/or prayer today.

Perform a random act of kindness today and post here:

Evening

What one thing went well today?

What one wish do you have for tomorrow?

The Daily Checklist

Complete this checklist every day for at least 21 days in a row.

Morning

Post three things you are grateful for today:

1

2

3

Select one behavioral strategy from Part 2 to use today and post here.

Get at least ten minutes of exercise today.

Take at least five minutes of quiet meditation and/or prayer today.

Perform a random act of kindness today and post here:

Evening

What one thing went well today?

What one wish do you have for tomorrow?

The Daily Checklist

Complete this checklist every day for at least 21 days in a row.

Morning

Post three things you are grateful for today:

    1

    2

    3

Select one behavioral strategy from Part 2 to use today and post here.

Get at least ten minutes of exercise today.

Take at least five minutes of quiet meditation and/or prayer today.

Perform a random act of kindness today and post here:

Evening

What one thing went well today?

What one wish do you have for tomorrow?

The Daily Checklist

Complete this checklist every day for at least 21 days in a row.

Morning

Post three things you are grateful for today:

1

2

3

Select one behavioral strategy from Part 2 to use today and post here.

Get at least ten minutes of exercise today.

Take at least five minutes of quiet meditation and/or prayer today.

Perform a random act of kindness today and post here:

Evening

What one thing went well today?

What one wish do you have for tomorrow?

The Daily Checklist

Complete this checklist every day for at least 21 days in a row.

Morning

Post three things you are grateful for today:

1

2

3

Select one behavioral strategy from Part 2 to use today and post here.

Get at least ten minutes of exercise today.

Take at least five minutes of quiet meditation and/or prayer today.

Perform a random act of kindness today and post here:

Evening

What one thing went well today?

What one wish do you have for tomorrow?

The Daily Checklist

Complete this checklist every day for at least 21 days in a row.

Morning

Post three things you are grateful for today:

1

2

3

Select one behavioral strategy from Part 2 to use today and post here.

Get at least ten minutes of exercise today.

Take at least five minutes of quiet meditation and/or prayer today.

Perform a random act of kindness today and post here:

Evening

What one thing went well today?

What one wish do you have for tomorrow?

The Daily Checklist

Complete this checklist every day for at least 21 days in a row.

Morning

Post three things you are grateful for today:

1

2

3

Select one behavioral strategy from Part 2 to use today and post here.

Get at least ten minutes of exercise today.

Take at least five minutes of quiet meditation and/or prayer today.

Perform a random act of kindness today and post here:

Evening

What one thing went well today?

What one wish do you have for tomorrow?

The Daily Checklist

Complete this checklist every day for at least 21 days in a row.

Morning

Post three things you are grateful for today:

1

2

3

Select one behavioral strategy from Part 2 to use today and post here.

Get at least ten minutes of exercise today.

Take at least five minutes of quiet meditation and/or prayer today.

Perform a random act of kindness today and post here:

Evening

What one thing went well today?

What one wish do you have for tomorrow?

The Daily Checklist

Complete this checklist every day for at least 21 days in a row.

Morning

Post three things you are grateful for today:

    1

    2

    3

Select one behavioral strategy from Part 2 to use today and post here.

Get at least ten minutes of exercise today.

Take at least five minutes of quiet meditation and/or prayer today.

Perform a random act of kindness today and post here:

Evening

What one thing went well today?

What one wish do you have for tomorrow?

The Daily Checklist

Complete this checklist every day for at least 21 days in a row.

Morning

Post three things you are grateful for today:

1

2

3

Select one behavioral strategy from Part 2 to use today and post here.

Get at least ten minutes of exercise today.

Take at least five minutes of quiet meditation and/or prayer today.

Perform a random act of kindness today and post here:

Evening

What one thing went well today?

What one wish do you have for tomorrow?

The Daily Checklist

Complete this checklist every day for at least 21 days in a row.

Morning

Post three things you are grateful for today:

1

2

3

Select one behavioral strategy from Part 2 to use today and post here.

Get at least ten minutes of exercise today.

Take at least five minutes of quiet meditation and/or prayer today.

Perform a random act of kindness today and post here:

Evening

What one thing went well today?

What one wish do you have for tomorrow?

The Daily Checklist

Complete this checklist every day for at least 21 days in a row.

Morning

Post three things you are grateful for today:

    1

    2

    3

Select one behavioral strategy from Part 2 to use today and post here.

Get at least ten minutes of exercise today.

Take at least five minutes of quiet meditation and/or prayer today.

Perform a random act of kindness today and post here:

Evening

What one thing went well today?

What one wish do you have for tomorrow?

ABOUT THE AUTHOR

Gail DePriest, MA

Gail brings over twenty years of experience in business management and leadership consulting. Having served as a Senior Vice President and Corporate Director in a global talent management firm, she has advised Fortune 500 companies and top ranked business schools. She is currently the Director of Corporate Relations & Leadership Development for Clemson University's College of Business and Behavioral Science.

She works with various organizations consulting for top performance and leadership excellence. DePriest is a certified Master Coach and is a contributing writer for the South Carolina Business Journal. She has worked with many organizations as an executive coach including Michelin, BMW and Wachovia. She has consulted with top-ranked business schools including Yale, Duke and George Washington School of Business.

Made in the USA
San Bernardino, CA
27 June 2014